CRYPTO WOJAK

The 10 Greatest Crypto Fails

A Laugh Through the Blockchain Jungle

Contents

Introduction   1

1 The $500 Million Pizza – Bitcoin's Tastiest Fail   5

2 Buried Bitcoins – The Hard Drive in the Landfill   11

3 The Vanishing CEO – The QuadrigaCX Crypto Mystery   16

4 The DAO Hack – When "Code is Law" Backfired   22

5 Mt. Goxxed – How to Lose 850,000 Bitcoins   28

6 Terra's Death Spiral – The Luna-Tic Stablecoin Crash   34

7 Silk Road – Crypto's Wild West Gets Busted   40

8 BitConnect – The Ponzi Scheme That Became a Meme   45

9 OneCoin – The Fake Crypto Pyramid and the Vanishing...   50

10 FailCoin – When a Joke Coin Got the Last Laugh   55

11 Bonus Chapter: Everyday Crypto Fails – Tales from the...   60

12 Conclusion   66

Introduction

Welcome to the blockchain jungle, dear reader. In this wild corner of the financial world, fortunes are made and lost faster than you can say "HODL." (If you're new here, that means "Hold On for Dear Life"—you'll pick up the lingo soon enough.) The cryptocurrency universe is a place where **truth is often stranger than fiction**. It's a realm of rocket emojis and meme coins, of overnight millionaires and sudden rug-pulls, where every triumph seems matched by an equally epic faceplant. **This book is about those faceplants**. And trust me, they're as educational as they are entertaining.

Pull up a seat (preferably a throne made of discarded crypto whitepapers) and prepare to dive into some of the craziest stories the crypto world has to offer. Ever hear about the guy who spent **10,000 Bitcoin on two pizzas**? Don't worry, you will—and yes, that number has *a lot* of zeros. Or how about the fellow who **threw away a hard drive** now worth half a billion dollars and has been *literally* digging through garbage to get it back? We'll get to him too. From vanished CEOs of crypto exchanges performing Houdini-level disappearing acts, to "stablecoins" that turned out to be as stable as nitroglycerin, we've got a bit of everything. Think of this as a guided tour of **Crypto's Hall of Fame (and Shame)**, with an emphasis on the shame.

Now, every jungle needs a guide. For our trek through the blockchain's untamed wilds, you'll be led by none other than **Crypto-Wojak**. Who's that, you ask? Picture the iconic internet meme character "Wojak" – that simple, line-drawn face that somehow perfectly captures the joy and pain of being a crypto investor. We've dressed him up in a cyberpunk hoodie, armed him with stacks of failed ICO tokens, and given him a mission: to comment on all the absurdity we're about to encounter. **Crypto-Wojak** is the voice of the crypto community – part wise old trader, part jaded "degen" (slang for *degenerate* gambler, the affectionate term crypto folks use for themselves when they YOLO into a bad trade). He'll be chiming in throughout the chapters to drop some sarcastic wisdom, meme-able one-liners, and maybe a coping mechanism or two for when things get *really* ridiculous.

Crypto-Wojak: "Buckle up, kiddos. I've got more scars from crypto than I have coins left in my wallet, and I'm here to make sure we all have a laugh about it."

As our snarky cartoon friend just hinted, this journey is all about **learning through laughter**. The tales you're about to read are not just urban legends whispered on Reddit (though some definitely are)—they're real events that have happened during the short but eventful life of cryptocurrencies. Each chapter delves into a monumental crypto mishap: the kind of blunder that makes you either cringe in sympathy or spit out your coffee laughing (or both, simultaneously—watch out, keyboards are expensive). We'll relive **Ten of the Greatest Crypto Fails** ever: from the infamous Bitcoin Pizza purchase and the

Mt. Gox hack, to Ponzi schemes like BitConnect and OneCoin that would make even Charles Ponzi himself say, "Dude, that's too far."

But hey, let's get one thing straight: **this is not a schadenfreude fest** (okay, maybe just a little). Sure, we're pointing and laughing at the train wrecks, but it's the kind of laughter you share with friends after surviving a crazy rollercoaster. The crypto community has a unique skill – when things go wrong, we meme about it, hard. Consider this book an extension of that coping strategy. For every person who lost money in these stories (and sadly, there are many), there's a lesson learned and a cautionary tale for the rest of us. Sometimes the lesson is obvious ("maybe don't put all your life savings in a coin literally named after a joke"), and sometimes it's more subtle ("decentralization is great, until you realize no one can hit the emergency stop button"). We promise to tease out those nuggets of wisdom amidst the chuckles.

Another thing: **this book is for entertainment purposes only**. Read that again, just in case the bold text didn't grab your attention. We are not here to give you financial advice or life advice—unless you count "maybe don't throw your only Bitcoin wallet in the trash" as life advice. By all means, learn from these epic fails, but remember, **Crypto-Wojak and friends are not your financial advisors**. (If they were, they'd have been fired long ago—did we mention the scars on Wojak's wallet?) So, no, we're not going to tell you how to get rich with crypto in ten easy steps. We're more about "how not to lose all your money in one hysterically misguided move."

Now that the lawyers are happy, let's talk about **you**, the reader. Perhaps you're a seasoned crypto veteran who rode out multiple boom-and-bust cycles, or maybe you're a curious newbie who just bought your first $50 of Bitcoin and heard it might be magic internet money. Either way, you're in for a treat. If you're a veteran, you'll laugh along and maybe even relive some PTSD (sorry!) from the good old days of Mt. Gox and BitConnect memes. If you're a newbie, consider this your informal *what-not-to-do* guide, wrapped in humor so it goes down easier. Think of it as getting inoculated against future mistakes— each story is a little vaccine of wisdom (with a sugar-coating of comedy).

By the end of our grand tour through crypto catastrophes, you'll not only be fluent in tales of crypto lore that will impress (or horrify) your friends at the next blockchain meetup, but you'll also appreciate how resilient this young industry is. I mean, after living through all of these disasters, **we're still here**, still building, still trading, and yes, still laughing. The crypto world, for all its dramas and absurdities, is one big experiment that *somehow* keeps bouncing back—much like Wile E. Coyote after a fall off a cliff, holding up a sign that says "Buy the Dip" as he plummets.

So, without further ado, tighten your seatbelt (we might experience some turbulence in these stories) and grab some popcorn (or avocado toast, if you're a true millennial). Just maybe don't order that popcorn with Bitcoin—at least, not until you finish Chapter 1 and see why it might not be the best idea **ever**.

One more thing before we start our adventure: remember that this journey is all in good fun. Real money and real people were involved in these fiascos, and our aim isn't to mock the pain of those who suffered. Rather, we shine a light on these **cautionary capers** to help everyone—ourselves included—learn and grow. Laughter can be the best medicine, especially when your crypto portfolio is feeling under the weather. As Crypto-Wojak would say:

Crypto-Wojak: "If you can't laugh at your own mistakes, make fun of someone else's and pretend it was them."

Alright, that's enough preamble. **The stage is set, the memes are primed, and Crypto-Wojak is ready with his sarcastic commentary.** Turn the page, and let's kick off this crazy journey through the *ten greatest crypto fails* of all time. Trust us, by the end you'll be laughing, learning, and maybe double-checking that you really did save your wallet backup. Let's roll!

1

The $500 Million Pizza – Bitcoin's Tastiest Fail

It all started with a **craving for pizza**. (Doesn't it always?) Back in May 2010, a Florida-based programmer named **Laszlo Hanyecz** was feeling a bit peckish. But he wasn't in the mood to pay for his two Papa John's pies with boring old dollars. Oh no, Laszlo had a stash of a then-obscure digital currency called Bitcoin, and he had an idea: *what if I use this magical internet money to get lunch?* So, on a historic day, May 18, 2010, Laszlo posted on an online forum:

"I'll pay 10,000 bitcoins for a couple of pizzas... like maybe 2 large ones so I have some left over for the next day."

At the time, **10,000 BTC was worth maybe $30 to $40**—roughly the cost of two delivered pizzas with a nice tip. Sounds like a fair trade, right? Keep in mind, Bitcoin was so new then that you couldn't exactly walk into Domino's and tap your phone to pay in crypto. Laszlo was proposing what amounted to a friendly trade: some generous soul orders him pizza to his door, and he sends them 10,000 BTC in return. It was a win-win: Laszlo gets his pepperoni fix, and the other person gets... well, a pile of digital coins that *might* be worth something someday.

> **Crypto-Wojak:** *"10,000 BTC for pizza? If I were around, I'd have delivered it* by plane *for that kind of money. (Of course, back then it was like trading Pokémon cards, not billions of dollars.)"*

For a few days, there were no takers. (Even in 2010, the idea of trading real food for imaginary coins made people a bit hesitant.) But eventually, on May 22, a willing counterparty emerged: a young British man named **Jeremy Sturdivant** (online alias "jercos") said, essentially, "Sure, why not?" Jeremy phoned in an order to Laszlo's local Papa John's for two large pizzas with the works, and in return, Laszlo transferred **10,000 BTC** to Jeremy's Bitcoin address. And just like that, **the first real-world Bitcoin transaction** was complete.

Laszlo gleefully posted an update on the forum: *"I just want to report that I successfully traded 10,000 Bitcoins for pizza."* He even shared pictures of the two sumptuous pies as proof of this milestone moment. Fellow forum members congratulated him, and Bitcoin Pizza Day was born. Yes, May 22 is now known as **Bitcoin Pizza Day**, celebrated every year by crypto enthusiasts worldwide (usually by eating pizza and then nervously calculating how much that pizza effectively "cost" them in missed future gains).

At the time, this was an exciting proof-of-concept. Bitcoin, which many had only seen traded for fun among a niche group of geeks, could actually buy something you could sink your teeth into! Laszlo was basically a pioneer, turning Bitcoin from an internet experiment into *real money*—at least for two delicious discs of dough, cheese, and tomato sauce.

Now fast forward a year: by 2011, Bitcoin hit $1 for the first time. Those 10,000 BTC were now worth $10,000. That's one pricey pizza party. Not many people knew about this little trade yet, but those who did started doing the mental math with each milestone Bitcoin crossed. When Bitcoin reached $100, suddenly we were talking **$1,000,000** worth of pizza. By late 2013, Bitcoin was around $1,000, making the pizzas a **$10 million meal**. The story started becoming legendary. Poor Laszlo! As Bitcoin kept climbing, the tale turned into the ultimate **"if only he had HODL'd"** parable.

Let's put this in perspective: **10,000 BTC** (the cost of Laszlo's two pizzas) is a fortune so large today that it defies pizza-related comprehension. At Bitcoin's peak price (around $69,000 in November 2021), those coins would have been worth roughly **$690 million**. Even at a more modest $30,000 per BTC, we're talking $300 million. In other words, each slice of pizza (assuming 16 slices total) ended up costing about **625 BTC** – or around **$18 million per slice** at $30k/BTC. Hope he savored each bite! Perhaps the most expensive toppings in history.

> *Crypto-Wojak:* "*I wonder if he paid extra for guacamole. Oh wait, wrong memeable commodity... Well, at these prices, I'd hope the pizza came with gold-plated pepperoni and a diamond-studded crust.*"

It's easy to poke fun in hindsight, but let's give Laszlo credit where it's due. At the time, **Bitcoin was practically play money.** Laszlo himself was a Bitcoin miner (one of the folks whose computers kept the network running and earned BTC as a reward). He reportedly mined tens of thousands of Bitcoin when it was easy to do so. For him, 10,000 BTC was no big deal—it was worth about what you'd spend on a nice dinner out. And he *really* wanted pizza. In a later interview, Laszlo insisted he had no regrets: someone had to kickstart the Bitcoin economy, and it might as well have been him. If nobody ever spent Bitcoin on real goods, would it ever have value? By trading those coins, he was proving a point: that crypto could be used in everyday life. (Though he probably didn't anticipate just how valuable those coins would become. Who could have?)

Fun fact: Laszlo actually continued to buy pizza with BTC a few more times after that first famous order, while Bitcoin's price was still negligible. He was basically saying, "Look, I'll do this anytime. Free pizza for anyone who wants to give me food in exchange for these funny internet coins!" Eventually, he stopped—perhaps as Bitcoin started gaining value (and perhaps at the urging of family members who were beginning to realize the *real* price of those pies!). In total, it's estimated he spent quite a lot of BTC on pizza that summer. In retrospect, you might think "Ouch, that's tens of millions per pepperoni by today's rates," but back then it kept him fed and helped spread the word about crypto.

The guy on the other end, Jeremy, got those 10,000 BTC. Surely **he** must be a billionaire now, right? Plot twist: Jeremy reportedly spent his Bitcoin stash on travel and living expenses, and possibly traded some for other investments. Like many early adopters, he didn't hold onto all of it for the long term. (One rumor is he sold them when BTC was still in the single digits. If true, he might have made a few thousand dollars. A great profit in 2010, but *facepalm*-worthy by 2020 standards.) It seems *nobody* in this story ended up insanely rich from that particular transaction. The universe has a sense of humor like that.

As the years passed and the legend grew, Bitcoin Pizza Day became a beloved **crypto holiday**. Every May 22nd, crypto fans commemorate Laszlo's expensive meal by sharing memes and, of course, buying pizzas—sometimes even with crypto if the pizzeria is savvy enough. (Some crypto companies run special promotions; one year you could get discounts on pizza if you paid in Bitcoin, which sort of brings it full circle.) There's even a plaque at a Papa John's in Florida to honor the infamous purchase, with an inscription: *"Papa John's – Makers of the Famous Bitcoin Pizzas. May 22, 2010."* Talk about a historic landmark for a fast-food chain!

This story encapsulates the **insanity of crypto gains**. How could anyone have known back then that those two piping hot pies would effectively cost more than a yacht, a mansion, and a private island *combined* a decade later? It's equal parts hilarious and heartbreaking, especially for Laszlo—though he genuinely maintains good humor about it. "I don't regret it," he's often said. "It's great to be part of Bitcoin's history." Talk about taking it in stride! If it were me, I'd have nightmares of a cartoon pizza slice laughing at me while dollar bills fluttered away in the breeze.

> **Crypto-Wojak:** *"Laszlo is a braver man than I. If I were him, every time someone said 'pizza' I'd probably burst into tears. Instead, he celebrates Bitcoin Pizza Day with the rest of us degenerates. Absolute legend."*

Fail-o-Meter: 7/10 (Hindsight is 20/20 – or in this case, 20 million. A monumental "oops" in dollar terms, but at least he got a tasty meal and a place in crypto history.)

Lessons Learned:

- *HODL (Hold On for Dear Life)* – Sometimes, holding onto your crypto instead of spending it can turn a humble purchase into a mind-blowing fortune. (In simpler terms: maybe think twice before trading all your coins for fast food, because you never know what they'll be worth later.)
- *Pioneers Pay a Price* – Early adopters often make sacrifices to prove a concept. Laszlo's purchase arguably helped legitimize Bitcoin as a real currency. No pain, no gain – for the community, if not for his personal net worth.
- *Don't Cry Over Spent Crypto* – Once a transaction is done, it's done. You never know how future markets will move. If you made a reasonable decision with the info you had at the time, try not to beat yourself up later. (Easier said than done when your $40 pizza becomes a $400 million pizza, but hey.)
- *Embrace the Meme* – The crypto world turned this apparent fail into a

positive, rallying point. Instead of ridiculing Laszlo, the community thanks him every year and has a laugh about it. Sometimes the best thing to do is lean into the absurdity and celebrate it.

2

Buried Bitcoins – The Hard Drive in the Landfill

In the quiet town of Newport, Wales, there lies a **landfill** filled with the usual rubbish: old furniture, broken electronics, banana peels, you name it. Unbeknownst to most, somewhere beneath all that trash is a *treasure* – a small hard drive containing **7,500 (or so) Bitcoin**. As of today, that's a haul worth hundreds of millions of dollars, just sitting there under layers of dirt and garbage. This isn't a plot from a movie – it's the real-life saga of **James Howells**, the IT guy who *accidentally threw away a fortune*.

Let's rewind to 2013. James Howells was an early Bitcoin miner. Back in 2009 and 2010, he had set up his personal laptop to mine BTC, back when you could do that without needing a nuclear-power-plant's worth of electricity. Over time, he amassed around 7,500 Bitcoin and stored the private keys on a small laptop hard drive. As Bitcoin was pretty much worthless then, James eventually stopped mining (possibly after spilling lemonade on the laptop – yes, that happened) and dismantled the parts. The hard drive with the Bitcoin sat forgotten in a drawer for a few years.

Fast-forward to mid-2013: James was doing some spring cleaning. In a moment that will haunt him forever, he threw out the *wrong* hard drive. Into the trash went the one containing his Bitcoin wallet keys. The drive got hauled off by the garbage collectors and ended up in Newport's **Docksway landfill**, buried under the daily deluge of local refuse. A few months later, Bitcoin's price started to soar. James suddenly remembered his stash – and realized with growing horror what he had done.

Imagine the sinking feeling: it's like realizing you left a winning lottery ticket in an old coat that you donated, except times a thousand. James had a **digital pot of gold** and he had literally tossed it in the garbage. When he did the math on what those coins were worth, he nearly fainted. At the time of realization, it was already in the millions of dollars. As Bitcoin kept climbing over the years, the value of that hard drive escalated from "house in the suburbs" to "private island and a yacht" levels.

> **Crypto-Wojak:** *"I've heard of burning money, but throwing it in the trash is a bold new strategy. BRB, going dumpster diving in Wales..."*

And thus began James Howells' epic quest to **recover his lost Bitcoin**. He wasn't going to just sit there while a fortune rotted away under old nappies and orange peels. He appealed to the local city council for permission to excavate the landfill. Now, landfills are not like those neat sand beaches where you can just grab a metal detector and start beeping around. We're talking about a massive expanse of waste, compacted and layered, likely with noxious gases wafting about. The hard drive by then was under **tons** of garbage, and possibly damaged – but *maybe not* entirely destroyed. After all, those Bitcoin private keys might still be on the platter if the drive hadn't been crushed.

The city council, however, was not keen on turning their landfill into a scene from *Indiana Jones and the Raiders of the Lost Ark*. They cited environmental risks, huge costs, and slim chances of success as reasons to deny his requests. James was persistent. Over the years, as Bitcoin's price skyrocketed, he came back to the council with ever more elaborate proposals. He offered them a percentage of the treasure (tens of millions of pounds) if they let him dig. He brought on investors and engineers, coming up with high-tech plans involving **robotic digging arms, AI-powered scanners, and even robot dogs** (yes, those fancy Boston Dynamics ones) to scour the landfill for that precious hard drive. It became a media sensation: the *modern-day treasure hunt* in a garbage dump.

Picture this: plans for a mechanized search effort combing through years of trash, with perhaps a team of hazmat-suited workers on standby. It's the stuff of a strangely compelling heist film – "The Great Bitcoin Dig". All the while, the clock is ticking because the longer the drive sits, the more it could corrode or be damaged by the elements (or by the compactor machines). James has often been quoted expressing a mix of hope and frustration: he's convinced the plan could work if only given the chance. The council remains unconvinced, imagining ecological disaster or a huge bill for a wild goose chase.

As of the latest chapters in this saga, **James still hasn't been allowed to search**. He's taken the fight to court, to the press, to anyone who will listen. But the landfill is effectively off-limits. It's as if the treasure is cursed – touching it might unleash some methane-monster or, more realistically, set a precedent for digging up landfills that the city really doesn't want. Recently, news broke that even a legal push was shot down; authorities finally told him to give up the dream. That hard drive will likely remain entombed in trash.

The tale of James Howells is both comical and tragic. On the one hand, it's hard not to chuckle at the absurdity of **millions of dollars worth of Bitcoin chilling next to old tea bags and garden clippings**. On the other hand, imagine being James: every time Bitcoin's price jumps, you'd feel physical pain. "There's my kid's college fund... sitting in a landfill. Oh, now it's a Ferrari... now it's a mansion... oh, now it's ten mansions." It's the ultimate lesson in the importance of **personal responsibility in crypto**. There's no customer support to call, no bank to reverse a transaction, and certainly no "undo" button for throwing away your private keys. If you lose access, it's gone.

James isn't alone, by the way. Plenty of early Bitcoin users have similar horror stories (though perhaps not involving literal landfills). Another famous example is a programmer who stored 7,002 BTC on an encrypted hard drive and *forgot the password*. He has two guesses left before the drive permanently encrypts the content, and he's shelved it in a secure facility for now, too scared to make another wrong attempt. There are also tales of people who threw away the paper where their wallet seed phrases were written, or accidentally sent Bitcoin to wrong addresses with no way back. In fact, analysts estimate that **around 20% of all Bitcoin is lost or stranded forever** due to mistakes and lost keys. James's story just happens to be the most cinematic.

> **Crypto-Wojak:** *"Not your keys, not your coins, as the saying goes. And in this case, not your keys because they're literally under about 10,000 tons of garbage. Ouch."*

Every now and then, when Bitcoin hits a new all-time high, reporters knock on James's door and ask, "So, about that hard drive..." He usually gives a rueful smile and reiterates that he hasn't given up hope. One can't help but root for him a little – the underdog (or under-trash?) story of a man determined to correct an epic blunder. If this were a Hollywood movie, he'd eventually get a call from the city saying "You have 48 hours to dig, go for it!", followed by a thrilling montage of excavation machines and dramatic music as they unearth the prize at the last second. Real life, sadly, isn't so generous.

So, as things stand, that hard drive remains buried. Maybe someday far in the future, archaeologists or treasure hunters with advanced tech will retrieve it and marvel at the primitive cryptocurrency within. Until then, James Howells will be the guy who might be a multi-millionaire in an alternate universe where he didn't take out the trash that day.

Fail-o-Meter: 9/10 (This is the stuff of legend and nightmares. A mind-blowing fortune lost in the most maddening way possible, with a slim chance of redemption.)

Lessons Learned:

- *Backup Your Wallet (For the Love of Crypto!)* – If you have cryptocurrency, **always back up your private keys and store them safely**. Preferably in multiple forms (digital and on paper) and in secure locations. Had James made an extra copy, he'd be relaxing on his private island now.
- *Be Careful What You Throw Away* – Today's junk might be tomorrow's treasure. In the digital age, that dusty hard drive or old USB stick could hold the keys to a fortune. Handle with care.
- *Not Your Keys, Not Your Coins* – A mantra in crypto: if you don't control the private keys, you don't truly own the coins. In James's case, he *had* the keys, then physically lost them. There's no central authority to appeal to. Self-sovereignty in finance is empowering but unforgiving of mistakes.
- *Fortune Favors the Prepared* – No one expects to throw out a lottery ticket. But taking a moment to plan for "what if" can save you from catastrophe. If you're diving into crypto, set up good habits (like safe storage) from day one.
- *Know When to Let Go?* – This one's tough, but sometimes chasing a loss can consume you. James's determination is admirable, but it's also eaten up years of his life. In crypto (and life), if a loss is truly irrecoverable, at some point you have to make peace and move on – or it will haunt you forever.

3

The Vanishing CEO – The QuadrigaCX Crypto Mystery

Our next tale plays out like a Netflix true-crime documentary (in fact, it became one). It's the story of **QuadrigaCX**, which was once Canada's largest cryptocurrency exchange, and its CEO **Gerald Cotten**. If you haven't heard this one, buckle up for a mystery filled with millions in missing crypto, a sudden death, and a boatload of unanswered questions.

In early 2019, users of QuadrigaCX got a shocking announcement: Gerald Cotten, the 30-year-old CEO, had **died suddenly** while on a trip to India. This was tragic in itself – but it came with an extra gut-punch for the exchange's 115,000 customers. According to the company, Cotten was the only person who had access to the exchange's cryptocurrency **cold wallets** (offline storage), and he had died *without sharing the passwords*. In other words, about **CAD $250 million (around US $190 million)** worth of Bitcoin, Ethereum, and other assets were supposedly locked away in accounts that no one else could open. Customers were told, effectively, "Sorry, we can't give you your money back – our only guy with the keys is gone."

Cue absolute pandemonium. People who had entrusted their life savings to QuadrigaCX were suddenly faced with the possibility that their money had vanished into the digital abyss. Initially, there was sympathy – "Oh no, the poor CEO died, how sad" – quickly followed by suspicion – "Wait, *he was the only one with the passwords? What kind of Mickey Mouse operation is this?!*" Then, as days passed with no sign of funds being recovered, the conspiracy theories ramped up to full throttle. The situation had more red flags than a bullfighters' convention.

Let's break down the absurdity: a major exchange (like a crypto bank, essentially) somehow had **zero contingency plan** for the loss of its CEO. Gerald Cotten apparently kept all the private keys to Quadriga's wallets in his **encrypted laptop**, and *no one else* in the company had access. No multi-signature accounts, no backups in a safe deposit box, nothing. It's as if a bank said, "Our vault? Yeah, only the CEO has the combination and, oops, he took it to the grave." Even by crypto's wild-west standards, this was a monumental operational fail.

Crypto-Wojak: "Rule #1 of crypto club: don't leave $190 million on a laptop that one dude takes on vacation. Rule #2: If Rule #1 is broken, at *least don't… you know, die with the password."*

As journalists and sleuths started digging, the Quadriga story got even crazier. For one, Gerald had written a **will just a month before his trip**, leaving everything to his new wife (they had just married) and even earmarking $100,000 for his two pet chihuahuas (yes, he planned for the dogs' future but apparently not the company's). Red flag? Perhaps. He died in India allegedly due to complications from Crohn's disease, but no one in the crypto community had known he was even ill. And here's the kicker: when investigators looked at the supposed "cold wallet" addresses where Quadriga's crypto was kept, they found **nothing there**. The wallets were empty. It appeared that the crypto had been missing well before Cotten's death was announced.

It turns out that QuadrigaCX was likely a house of cards. A post-mortem (pardon the phrase) investigation by the Canadian securities regulators later concluded that **Quadriga was basically running a Ponzi scheme** by the end. Gerald Cotten had been trading with customer funds, losing a bunch on risky bets and bad crypto investments. He created fake accounts under aliases (one amusing alias: "Scepter") on his own exchange to conjure fake profits, and would use new deposits to pay out older customers who wanted withdrawals – classic Ponzi behavior. By the time of his death, there was a massive shortfall. In plain terms: the money was gone, long gone, and his passing was either the unfortunate event that exposed the fraud or (as some theorize) a convenient cover-up.

Yes, there are **wild theories that Gerald faked his own death** to abscond with what remained of the money. After all, he died in India (where, sensational speculators like to note, fake death certificates can be had for the right price), and only one death certificate was issued by a local hospital. The body was quickly embalmed and flown back to Canada. Skeptics asked: why wasn't there a proper autopsy in Canada? Why did he go to India in the first place (reportedly to open an orphanage, if the story is to be believed)? And wouldn't it be just the plot twist to have him sipping a cocktail on some beach under a new identity?

To be clear, no concrete evidence has emerged that Cotten is alive. It might just be that he died at a very inconvenient time – right when his business was collapsing. The timing is either incredibly bad luck or incredibly *convenient*. Either way, over a hundred million dollars of customer funds were gone, and people were (understandably) furious.

The fallout was ugly. QuadrigaCX went bankrupt, of course. Lawyers, regulators, and blockchain forensic experts got involved to trace whatever funds they could. They did find a few coins in some wallets (a negligible amount) and discovered that Cotten had moved a lot of crypto to other exchanges (likely cashing out or trading). His widow, **Jennifer Robertson**, claimed to have no idea about the shady dealings and said she also lost everything (aside from the assets in the will, which included properties, a small airplane, and the famous chihuahuas' trust fund). She eventually agreed to return about $12 million of assets to help repay creditors – a drop in the bucket compared to the overall hole.

The incident rocked the crypto world. Here was an exchange that had been in operation for years, seemingly legit, and it all came down to one guy who had everyone's trust – and he blew it (either through malfeasance, negligence, or both). It underscored the rallying cry that crypto veterans always preach: **"Not your keys, not your coins."** If you leave your crypto on an exchange, you are trusting someone else to guard it. And if that someone is essentially running a one-man show and is secretly a goof (or a crook), well, you could end up like Quadriga's customers: out in the cold.

> **Crypto-Wojak:** *"I had coins on Quadriga. When I heard the news, I went through all five stages of grief in about thirty minutes, then got stuck somewhere between anger and facepalming disbelief."*

The Quadriga fiasco is often referred to as one of crypto's biggest scandals. It's got everything: mystery, fraud, a death (or disappearance), and loads of meme-worthy disbelief. There's a popular meme image of a gravestone that reads: "R.I.P. Passwords – Taken by Gerald Cotten." Another shows Scooby-Doo unmasking a villain, with Gerald's face under the mask saying "It was me, Satoshi, all along!" (Crypto folks have a dark sense of humor.)

Jokes aside, the human impact was real. Some folks lost significant savings. Legal proceedings to recover whatever scraps remain are ongoing, but creditors (the users) have only gotten back a small fraction of what they had on the exchange. Many will likely never be made whole.

So what do we make of this? If it's a genuine tragedy – a young CEO dies and, through poor planning, locks up everyone's money – then it's a cautionary tale of extreme mismanagement. If it's an elaborate scam, then it's a cautionary tale of extreme misplaced trust. Either way: **big fail**. Exchanges around the world took note and started implementing "dead man switches" and better key management after this. And users took note too: diversifying where you keep funds, and preferably holding your own coins in a personal wallet, started to look a lot more attractive after Quadriga's fall.

Perhaps one day the full truth will come out – maybe an exhumation of Cotten's body (some investors demanded this, seriously!), or a surprise reappearance. Until then, QuadrigaCX remains a modern crypto mystery and a lesson etched in the blockchain's lore.

Fail-o-Meter: 10/10 (Whether by death, deception, or both – losing $190 million of other people's money is a 10 on the fail scale. This one scores extra for the "are you kidding me?!" factor.)

Lessons Learned:

- *Not Your Keys, Not Your Coins (Reprise)* – This phrase bears repeating. If you leave your crypto on an exchange, you're trusting someone else completely. If they screw up or run off, you're out of luck. Use reputable exchanges and even then, consider withdrawing to your own wallet for long-term holds.
- *Have a Contingency Plan* – If you run any financial platform, **never** design it so that one person is a single point of failure. Bus factor of one (meaning if one person gets hit by a bus, everything breaks) is a colossal management fail. Share access, use multi-sig, have backups. Cotten's team apparently

didn't – and look what happened.

- *Due Diligence and Skepticism* – The Quadriga case reminds us to do some homework on where we put our money. If an exchange's operation seems too opaque or hinges on a single charismatic figure, be cautious. Sometimes even regulators and users got fooled, but keep that skeptic radar on.
- *Expect the Unexpected* – No one thought "CEO might die with all the passwords" was a risk to worry about – until it happened. In crypto (and life), sometimes black-swan events occur. Spread out your risk. Don't put all your eggs (or coins) in one basket (or one exchange).
- *Trust No One (Literally)* – This was actually the subtitle of a documentary on this saga: *Trust No One*. In crypto, that phrase resonates. The technology is built to eliminate the need for trust via verification. Use that to your advantage. It's not about being paranoid; it's about being smart with your money in a realm where mistakes and fraud can happen.

4

The DAO Hack – When "Code is Law" Backfired

In 2016, the Ethereum community attempted a bold experiment in decentralized governance and finance. They created "The DAO" (short for Decentralized Autonomous Organization), essentially a leaderless investment fund managed entirely by code and voting from its token holders. Think of it as a venture capital fund run by robots on the blockchain – what could possibly go wrong? Well, **$60 million worth of ETH could go wrong**, as we found out. The DAO hack is a legendary tale of idealism meeting reality, where a clever attacker said, "Thank you very much for your flawed smart contract, I'll be taking those funds now," and nearly blew a hole in Ethereum itself.

Let's set the scene: The DAO was launched in April 2016 after a huge crowdfunding on Ethereum. It was the biggest crowdfunding effort at the time – about **12.7 million Ether** was raised from thousands of excited people who wanted to be part of this futuristic investment club. At the time, that Ether was worth around $150 million. (In retrospect, at later prices that would be billions – you'll notice a trend in these chapters: early sums of crypto that later become massive). The idea was that DAO token holders would propose and vote on projects to invest in, and if those projects made profits, the profits would flow back into The DAO and thus to its investors. It was all run by smart contracts – self-executing code on Ethereum. No CEOs, no board of directors, just code and votes. **"Code is law,"** the saying went – meaning the rules of the smart contract are the ultimate authority.

But code, like law, can have loopholes. And boy, did The DAO have a loophole. In June 2016, someone discovered a vulnerability in The DAO's smart contract – specifically a *"reentrancy"* bug, if you're technically inclined – which basically allowed them to withdraw funds repeatedly from The DAO before the smart contract updated the balance. It's like if an ATM let you keep withdrawing money from an account by tricking it into not updating your balance after each withdrawal. On **June 17, 2016**, the attacker (or attackers) struck. They initiated a withdrawal from The DAO, and then recursively called the withdraw function over and over, **siphoning about 3.6 million ETH** into a "child DAO" – which was essentially an account controlled by them.

Panic ensued across the Ethereum community. This was a catastrophe: roughly a third of The DAO's funds were being stolen in real time. People on forums and chat rooms were watching in horror as the Ethereum blockchain showed chunk after chunk of Ether flowing to the attacker's address. It was like watching a bank heist in slow motion, in broad daylight, on an immutable ledger. Due to the way The DAO was structured, those funds were now in the hacker's own mini-DAO, but with a catch: according to the DAO's rules, withdrawals from that child DAO couldn't be finalized for 28 days. So the Ether was snatched but couldn't be moved off-chain immediately – a small silver lining buying time for a response.

The Ethereum developers and community had an existential crisis to resolve. Option 1: do nothing, accept that "code is law," and let the hacker potentially walk away with a huge chunk of Ethereum's total supply when the 28 days passed (which could severely damage trust in the platform). Option 2: intervene by somehow undoing or mitigating the hack. But intervening meant violating the principle of blockchain immutability – effectively admitting that code might *not* be the only law if enough people agree to change it. This was unprecedented stuff. Debates raged: *Should Ethereum hard fork (i.e., create a network update that rewinds the hack)? Would that destroy credibility or save the platform?* It was the decentralization equivalent of an ethics trolley problem.

Ultimately, the majority of the community (including Ethereum's creator, Vitalik Buterin) chose to **hard fork**. In July 2016, they executed a fork that essentially moved the stolen ETH from the attacker's address into a new smart contract that allowed the original DAO investors to withdraw it back, as if the hack never happened. This fork created a split: the main Ethereum network (ETH) went on as if the hack was reverted, while a faction of purists who opposed the fork stuck with the old chain, which became known as **Ethereum Classic (ETC)**. On Ethereum Classic, the hacker's haul remained in their control (oh hello, parallel universe where the robber got away clean).

The hacker, by the way, wasn't quietly twiddling thumbs during all this. In a bizarre twist, they (or someone claiming to be them) publicly declared that they had taken the Ether "fair and square" according to the rules of the contract – after all, they just executed the code that was there – and even offered a sort of bribe: they'd give a chunk back if they got to keep some. They also threatened legal action if their "legal right" to the funds was infringed by a fork. Imagine a bank robber writing a letter to the cops saying, "Actually, the vault door was open, and your bank rules allowed me to take the money, so it's mine now. If you interfere, I'll sue!" It was equal parts brazen and absurd. Needless to say, the community went ahead with the fork anyway.

> **Crypto-Wojak:** "Only in crypto do you have thousands of people voting on whether to hit the giant undo button on a $60 million hack while the hacker is in the background yelling, 'This is against the rules!' What a time to be alive."

The hard fork was implemented and the stolen funds were restored to the DAO token holders (in Ether on the new fork). Most participants moved on with Ethereum as we know it today. However, Ethereum Classic still exists as a smaller, separate network – carrying the original history (including the hack). The hacker, or whoever holds those keys, ended up with a lot of ETC (Ethereum Classic coins), which, due to the split and market dynamics, became worth far less than the equivalent ETH on the main chain. It's poetic in a way: they aimed to steal the crown jewels, but ended up with the discount-bin version of them.

The DAO itself was kaput. It was quickly shut down after the hack and refund process. The grand experiment ended in failure. *The name "The DAO" became almost taboo for a while in Ethereum circles.* (Nowadays "DAO" just refers generically to decentralized organizations, but you'll still see old-timers get a twitch in their eye at the mention of The DAO.) For Ethereum, it was a painful lesson. It showed that smart contracts, once deployed, are only as perfect as the code they contain – and if there's a mistake, the consequences are dire. It also proved that the community could come together to address a crisis, but at the cost of breaking a principle, which still fuels debates at crypto conferences: "Was it right to fork?"

Many argued that if Ethereum hadn't forked, the platform might have lost credibility (who wants to build on something where an obvious exploit was allowed to stand?). Others argued the fork undermined the very trustlessness and immutability that blockchains are supposed to have. There's no easy answer – both viewpoints have merit, which is exactly why Ethereum and

Ethereum Classic both have their supporters to this day.

For the purposes of our fail-o-rama, The DAO hack stands out as a *technological* fail. Unlike the other chapters, this wasn't a scam or human folly in the traditional sense; it was a bug in code that had huge ramifications. But the chaos and drama that followed, and the sheer scale of value at stake, cement it as one of the great crypto fails.

It's also sprinkled with irony: a venture fund meant to democratize and decentralize finance ended up nearly sinking the very platform it was built on, requiring a very *centralized* decision (by developers and community voting) to save the day. The joke "DAO = **Dead On Arrival**" made the rounds afterward. And for a while, the phrase "code is law" was said with a sarcastic snicker – because apparently, sometimes the law gets vetoed by an even higher power: consensus of the community to fix a giant mess.

In the aftermath, Solidity (the language used for Ethereum contracts) and smart contract development practices got a lot more scrutiny. "Audits" became a must-do for any serious project. The concept of **bug bounties** (paying hackers to find bugs ethically before launch) gained traction. In a way, Ethereum grew up a lot because of The DAO hack. It was a costly learning experience, but it led to much better security awareness. To this day, though, whenever someone proposes a new big ambitious DAO project, the ghost of The DAO hovers in the background, whispering, "Are you sure that code is safe, fren?"

Fail-o-Meter: 8/10 (A high-profile disaster that shook Ethereum to its core. Not a total loss thanks to the community rollback, but it literally split a blockchain and forever altered the "code is law" narrative.)

Lessons Learned:

- *Audit Your Smart Contracts* – If you're going to lock up a gazillion dollars in a self-executing program, you'd better have that code **triple-audited** by security experts. The DAO had a known vulnerability that wasn't fixed in time. In crypto, one tiny bug can cost millions.

- *Code is Law... Until It Isn't* – The DAO hack showed that there are limits to the "immutable ledger" principle. The community's decision to fork was controversial, but many felt it was necessary. The lesson: decentralized systems still ultimately have people behind them, and they may intervene in extreme cases. Purists will debate it forever.
- *Don't Put All Your Eggs in One DAO* – The DAO was an exciting experiment, but putting so much money into an unproven smart contract was asking for trouble. Diversification of risk applies in crypto too: maybe don't shove a huge percentage of a blockchain's economy into a single new contract that hasn't been battle-tested.
- *Resilience in Crisis* – Even when catastrophic fails happen, a strong community can sometimes band together to set things right (or as right as possible). Ethereum didn't crumble; it adapted. This is a reassuring lesson: big fails don't have to be the end, if people work toward a solution.
- *Innovate Carefully* – The DAO was cutting-edge, but perhaps rushed. The fail teaches a balance: innovation is great, but when dealing with real money, caution and thorough testing are your friends. The frontier of blockchain is exciting, but it's also littered with the wreckage of "move fast and break things" projects. Better to move a *little* slower and break nothing.

5

Mt. Goxxed – How to Lose 850,000 Bitcoins

If you were involved in crypto back in the early 2010s, the name **Mt. Gox** still sends a shiver down your spine. This was the first *and* arguably the most infamous cryptocurrency exchange disaster. It was such a defining fiasco that the slang "to get Goxxed" became synonymous with losing money due to an exchange collapse or hack. So what was Mt. Gox? And how did it manage to lose a literal mountain of Bitcoin?

Funny enough, **Mt. Gox started as a trading platform for Magic: The Gathering cards**. (Yes, the nerdy card game – in fact "Mt. Gox" is short for "Magic: The Gathering Online eXchange".) It was later repurposed around 2010 as one of the first Bitcoin exchanges. In the wild early days of Bitcoin, Mt. Gox quickly grew to handle *the majority* of Bitcoin trading globally. By 2013, it was *the* place to buy and sell BTC; some estimates say it handled around 70% of all Bitcoin transactions at its peak. If you were into Bitcoin, you likely had an account on Mt. Gox.

The exchange was run out of Tokyo by a somewhat eccentric Frenchman named **Mark Karpelès**. Mark was a programmer, known online as "MagicalTux". He was brilliant in some ways but perhaps not the world's most organized CEO. He was also a cat lover who often live-tweeted about his fat feline (named Tibanne – which even became the name of his holding company). This picture-perfect setup – an anime-loving guy with a cat running a half-a-billion-dollar exchange out of a small office – what could go wrong? Well, in hindsight, *a lot*.

Mt. Gox had a series of issues throughout its life: security breaches, banking problems (accounts getting frozen), and a general lack of transparency. But things truly unraveled in February 2014. Users had been complaining about withdrawal delays for weeks. Then, abruptly, Mt. Gox halted all Bitcoin withdrawals, blaming a technical issue (they cited a "transaction malleability" bug in Bitcoin – a real quirk, but one that other exchanges were handling without catastrophic problems). As users panicked, the site went dark. On February 28, 2014, Mt. Gox filed for bankruptcy protection in Japan. Karpelès announced that **approximately 850,000 BTC were missing** and presumed stolen – at the time, worth about $450 million. It was, and remains, one of the largest losses of Bitcoins ever.

To put 850,000 BTC in perspective: at Bitcoin's later prices, that's tens of billions of dollars. Even at the time, $450 million was a devastating amount, both in real money and as a chunk of Bitcoin's total market cap. How on earth did so many coins vanish? Mt. Gox claimed it was hackers – that over the years, thieves had been siphoning bitcoins out of their hot wallets without being noticed. Critics argue that it was a mix of hacking and sheer mismanagement. Either way, customers were suddenly left with their account balances showing zeros.

The reaction in the crypto world ranged from outrage to utter despair. Online, people posted memes of the Mt. Gox logo sinking like the Titanic. Others made images of a wizard (a nod to Magic: The Gathering) making bitcoins disappear with a wand. Some Mt. Gox customers protested outside the company's office in Tokyo, holding signs (in English and Japanese) demanding their money. It was chaotic.

One somewhat comedic detail: after the bankruptcy, in a twist, **200,000 BTC were "found" in an old-format wallet** that Mt. Gox had forgotten about (talk about checking your couch cushions and finding $100 million in loose change!). That reduced the unrecovered amount to about 650,000 BTC, but by then, the damage was done. Years of legal proceedings followed. Mt. Gox became a byword for crypto disaster.

Mark Karpelès himself became a controversial figure. Some angry customers accused him of fraud, others of incompetence. He maintained that Mt. Gox was hacked and he did nothing criminal. The Japanese authorities eventually arrested him in 2015 – not for the hack, but on charges of embezzlement and data manipulation. He spent months in detention. In 2019, he was cleared of embezzling funds (they didn't find evidence he stole money for himself) but was convicted on a lesser charge of falsifying records (basically, he had fiddled with Mt. Gox's database to hide the fact they were insolvent). He received a suspended sentence (meaning he didn't go back to prison, as long as he stayed out of trouble). In the court of public opinion, however, Mark will forever be the guy at the helm when the biggest pile of Bitcoin ever went poof.

Crypto-Wojak: "I still have Mt. Gox PTSD. Anytime an exchange is slow to process a withdrawal, my brain screams 'Goxxed!'. The struggle is real."

For those victims, there is a semi-bright spot at the end of this tunnel (a decade later). The bankruptcy process has been ongoing, and because the remaining 200k Bitcoins ballooned in value over the years, even after paying off creditors in fiat terms, there's leftover value to distribute. In fact, oddly, some Mt. Gox creditors might end up getting back an amount equal to or even more (in dollar terms) than they lost, thanks to Bitcoin's huge price increase since 2014. However, it's been a painfully slow wait. As of the time of writing, final distributions are only just starting to happen – more than ten years since the collapse. Patience is a virtue; patience while watching Bitcoin skyrocket knowing yours are locked in legal limbo – that's torture.

The Mt. Gox collapse taught the crypto community several hard lessons (many learned the phrase **"Not your keys, not your coins"** from this event, as in, if you don't hold the private keys, you're trusting someone else to secure your coins). It spurred improvements in exchange security. Nowadays, major exchanges keep the majority of funds in cold storage, use audits, and have all sorts of safeguards to avoid being "the next Mt. Gox". In a way, Mt. Gox crawled so modern exchanges could walk (hopefully not faceplant).

Culturally, the Gox saga left a mark. Even years later, whenever an exchange has withdrawal issues or rumors of insolvency, the ghost of Mt. Gox looms: panicked users say "Is this another Gox? Should I pull my funds?" The tale is retold to every crypto newbie at some point, usually with a moral attached. You see a person with a crypto T-shirt that says "Mt. Gox Alumni" or "I got Goxxed" – it's dark humor, commemorating membership in a club no one wanted to join.

The phrase "magic internet money" ironically literalized at Mt. Gox – a huge amount of money did a magic disappearing act. Was it incompetence, internal malfeasance, external hackers, or all of the above? Probably a mix, but the end result is the same: people lost trust and money. Mt. Gox's demise likely slowed down Bitcoin's adoption for a while, as headlines blared about the "collapse of Bitcoin" and skeptics crowed that it was the end (spoiler: it wasn't).

If nothing else, Mt. Gox provided the archetype of what **not** to do as a crypto exchange and hammered home to users the importance of being careful where you park your crypto assets. It's a cautionary legend that will be told around digital campfires for decades.

Fail-o-Meter: 10/10 (Losing a vast fortune of user funds and nearly taking Bitcoin down with it? Yep, that's a full 10. This is the OG mega-fail that still haunts crypto history.)

Lessons Learned:

- *Not Your Keys, Not Your Coins (Yet Again)* – This mantra was practically born from the ashes of Mt. Gox. If you don't control the private keys to your crypto (i.e., if it's on an exchange), you're trusting someone else's security and honesty. That someone might be great... until they aren't. Consider personal wallets for long-term holding.
- *Security First, Second, and Third* – For exchanges and any crypto business, security must be an obsession. Mt. Gox's security was clearly lacking (e.g., leaving too many coins in hot wallets, possibly weak internal controls). Today's exchanges are far more security-conscious as a direct response to this disaster.
- *Transparency and Accountability* – Users had very little insight into Mt. Gox's internal health until it was too late. Modern exchanges learned to provide more transparency (proof-of-reserves audits, public communication, etc.). If you're using an exchange that's opaque and dodgy about issues, be wary.
- *Don't Put All Your Bitcoins in One Basket* – Many folks had *all* their Bitcoin on Mt. Gox because it was convenient. Diversify your risk: maybe keep some on an exchange for trading, but store the rest in a hardware wallet or split among platforms. That way, one failure won't wipe you out completely.
- *Learn from History* – The crypto world changes fast, but we shouldn't forget the past. Every time a new wave of users comes in, the veterans dutifully share Mt. Gox war stories to instill a bit of healthy caution. The

takeaway: yes, crypto is exciting and can be lucrative, but never assume that any platform is infallible. Stay alert, and keep your wits (and your coins) about you.

6

Terra's Death Spiral – The Luna-Tic Stablecoin Crash

In the annals of "this was supposed to be stable," no story stands out quite like the 2022 crash of **TerraUSD (UST)** and its sister token **Luna**. It was a collapse so dramatic that it wiped out around **$40 billion** in value and sent shockwaves throughout the crypto market. It's the tale of a so-called stablecoin that proved anything but stable, and an egotistic founder who flew too close to the sun (or rather, the moon) and got burned.

Let's unpack this in plain English: **UST was an algorithmic stablecoin** on the Terra blockchain, designed to maintain a 1:1 peg with the US dollar without being fully backed by actual dollars. Instead, it used a kind of seesaw mechanism with Terra's native token, **Luna**. In theory, if UST drifted below $1, you could swap UST for $1 worth of Luna (which would be destroyed in the process) – reducing UST supply and pushing its price back up. Conversely, if UST went above $1, you could swap $1 of Luna for 1 UST (creating more UST and bringing price down). This arbitrage was supposed to keep UST at $1 automatically. The whole system relied on the market's confidence that Luna had value and that people would want UST.

For a while, it worked. Actually, it more than worked – it boomed. By early 2022, UST had become the third-largest stablecoin, and Luna's price was soaring. A big reason: the **Anchor Protocol**, a sort of savings account on Terra, promised a whopping **20% APY** on UST deposits. 20% interest on a "stable" asset? In a world of near-zero bank interest, that was like a magnet for crypto investors. Billions of UST flowed into Anchor from folks chasing that yield. Everything looked fantastic... until it didn't.

Enter **Do Kwon**, the brash South Korean co-founder of Terra. Do Kwon was the public face of the project and had a reputation for being, let's say, *extremely confident* (bordering on cocky). He routinely dismissed critics on Twitter with insults, calling them "poor" or claiming they were dumb for doubting him. He famously quipped "I don't debate the poor" and responded to someone warning of UST's vulnerability with "Your size is not size" (basically telling them they're too insignificant to matter). In hindsight, this arrogance was a huge red flag – kind of like a tech CEO in 2007 saying their subprime mortgage-backed securities are unbeatable (what could go wrong?).

The collapse began in May 2022. UST started to slip from its $1 peg – just a few cents at first. Normally that arbitrage mechanism should kick in. But something was different this time: confidence was wavering. Whether due to a coordinated attack (some theories suggest big players shorted UST and sold a ton to break the peg) or just a panic, UST kept drifting down. It fell to $0.90... then $0.80. People began to lose trust. A so-called stablecoin at 80 cents is like seeing a canary in a coal mine keel over. Everyone rushed for the exit. To defend UST's peg, huge amounts of Luna were being minted and sold to buy UST — but that tanked Luna's price, which in turn eroded confidence further in the whole system backing UST. This was the dreaded **death spiral**.

Picture a vicious cycle: UST price drops -> more Luna is created to try to stabilize UST -> Luna price plummets due to dilution and panic -> Luna's drop makes UST even less credible -> UST holders dump even harder -> rinse and repeat. It was like watching a slow-motion car crash that suddenly turns into a full-speed pileup.

Do Kwon initially tried to calm the masses. On Twitter he famously wrote, "*Steady lads, deploying more capital.*" That tweet instantly became legend (in the worst way possible) because shortly after, "steady" gave way to total freefall. The Luna Foundation Guard (an organization set up to help protect UST's peg, which had amassed a reserve of Bitcoin and other assets for emergencies) did deploy billions worth of Bitcoin to buy UST — but it was like trying to plug a collapsing dam with your finger. Within a span of just *a few days*, **UST imploded from $1 to under 10 cents**, and **Luna... oh, Luna** — Luna, which had been over $80 per coin in early May, literally cratered to fractions of a penny by mid-May. It wasn't just a crash; it was an extinction-level event for the Terra ecosystem.

The speed of this collapse was mind-boggling. Imagine going to bed thinking you have $100,000 in "stable" UST (and maybe dreaming of that sweet 20% yield you'll earn), and waking up to find it's worth $15,000 and plummeting. People were in disbelief. Some thought it must be a bug on the price feed. It wasn't. Real money was evaporating. Online forums filled with horror stories: life savings lost, houses mortgaged to buy Luna or UST now gone, college funds vaporized. There were even reports of suicides, which is absolutely heart-wrenching. The human toll was real.

The aftermath: Terra's blockchain was halted. The community (what was left of it) and Do Kwon decided to abandon UST entirely and try to salvage something by forking the blockchain into a new one. A new coin, Terra 2.0 (LUNA) was created and airdropped to some of the victims – but without the stablecoin component. The original chain was rebranded as Terra Classic, with Luna Classic (LUNC) and UST Classic (USTC) still trading at tiny values, mostly for speculators and meme value. Essentially, Terra as it was known died in that crash.

As for Do Kwon, the consequences came knocking. The South Korean authorities launched investigations, since many Korean citizens were affected. It turned out TerraForm Labs (Kwon's company) had been told by some in the know that the model might fail and allegedly even had an internal version called "basis cash" that already failed – hinting they knew the risks. Do Kwon left South Korea (some say fled). By late 2022, South Korea issued an arrest warrant for him, and Interpol put out a Red Notice. He became a crypto fugitive, occasionally popping up on Twitter to deny he was "on the run" (though he clearly was avoiding jurisdictions with extradition). In early 2023, he was reportedly arrested in Montenegro attempting to travel with fake documents. Legal proceedings await him in multiple countries; he could face serious prison time if convicted of fraud or other charges.

The Terra/Luna fiasco shook the entire crypto industry. It caused a broader crash in mid-2022, as confidence in other stablecoins and projects wavered. It also drew regulatory attention – regulators were like, "See, this is what happens in the Wild West of crypto, we need to rein this in." There's now talk of stablecoin regulations to prevent something like UST from ever getting that big and unregulated again.

From a learnings perspective, this fail hammered home a few points. One, if something offers **insanely high returns with "no risk,"** question it. Anchor's 20% yields were subsidized by the Terra project's funds – basically a marketing gimmick that wasn't sustainable. It was like a honey pot to lure in capital, and once that subsidy ran out or confidence wavered, down it all went. Two, **algorithmic stablecoins** had a history of failure even before Terra (several smaller ones had death-spiraled too). Terra was just the biggest and most confident. The inherent issue: they rely on perpetual market confidence;

once that's gone, there's no floor. It's a bit like an umbrella that evaporates when it rains.

> **Crypto-Wojak:** *"I admit it, I was in Anchor earning that juicy 20% on UST. I told myself, 'Banks are dumb, this is the future of savings!' Then I watched my 'safe' savings implode faster than you can say 'UST in peace'. I've never moved back to boring bank accounts so fast in my life."*

This story also highlighted how charismatic leaders can lead an entire community off a cliff. Do Kwon's online persona (brash, confident) actually attracted a lot of fans who thought he was a genius who would make them all rich. It became almost cult-like – they called themselves "Lunatics" (a term originally meant in fun, which aged like milk). After the crash, many of those believers felt deeply betrayed.

In the end, the Terra/Luna collapse joins the pantheon of great crypto fails due to its sheer scale and the hubris involved. It's a cautionary tale that will be cited every time someone proposes a new algorithmic stablecoin or whenever a crypto project leader starts smelling a bit too much like snake oil. As the saying now goes: **"Steady lads, maybe don't deploy that capital so fast."**

Fail-o-Meter: 10/10 (A multi-billion dollar vaporization of supposedly stable assets, leaving a trail of financial ruin. This fail scores full marks on scale, shock, and the "should've seen it coming" irony.)

Lessons Learned:

- *If It Sounds Too Good (20% APY Risk-Free), It Probably Is* – High yields in crypto often come with hidden risks. Anchor's 20% APY on UST was too good to be true long-term. Always ask: where is this yield coming from? In this case, it was essentially venture capital fuel that ran out. Skepticism can save you a lot of money.
- *Algorithmic Stablecoins = High Risk* – History has shown that stablecoins without solid collateral (be it fiat or overcollateralized crypto) are fragile.

Be extremely wary of any "stable" asset that isn't transparently backed. The word "stablecoin" doesn't guarantee stability – Terra's UST proved that emphatically.

- *Beware of Cult Personalities* – Don't let a founder's confidence trick you into ignoring red flags. Do Kwon's swagger convinced many that "this time is different." It wasn't. Healthy skepticism of charismatic leaders is warranted – ask hard questions, demand transparency.

- *Diversify and Take Profits* – Many who got into Luna early saw huge gains on paper… and then rode it all the way back down. It's important to take profits and not concentrate everything in one project, no matter how bulletproof it seems. Spread out risk – maybe some in Bitcoin, some in more proven stablecoins, etc. – so one collapse doesn't wreck your entire portfolio.

- *Regulations Aren't All Evil* – While crypto folks often disdain regulation, Terra's collapse shows why some oversight can be helpful. If a stablecoin is large enough to hurt many people when it fails, maybe there should be transparency or capital requirements. At least, as an investor, seek projects that practice self-regulation (audits, transparency, etc.). A bit of caution from regulators or industry standards might prevent the next Terra.

7

Silk Road – Crypto's Wild West Gets Busted

Time to take a detour into the dark side of crypto – literally, the dark web. In the early 2010s, Bitcoin gained a bit of a sketchy reputation, largely thanks to **Silk Road**, the notorious online marketplace where you could buy just about any illegal thing you desired, all with Bitcoin, and (supposedly) anonymously. It was like Amazon... if Amazon sold narcotics, fake IDs, and weapons, and only accepted crypto.

The **Silk Road** website launched in 2011, accessible only via the Tor network (an anonymity network that hides your IP). It was the brainchild of a Texan named **Ross Ulbricht**, who ran it under the pseudonym "Dread Pirate Roberts" (a reference to *The Princess Bride* – indicating perhaps that the persona could be passed on to others). His vision was a free-market utopia (or dystopia, depending on your view) where people could trade freely without government interference. And trade they did – mostly drugs at first. Sellers and buyers flocked to Silk Road, drawn by the promise of anonymity. Bitcoin was the grease that made this underground economy possible: a digital cash that, in those days, many assumed was untraceable.

For a while, Silk Road thrived. It had thousands of listings and did millions of dollars in sales. It was like a digital speakeasy that authorities knew about but had trouble shutting down because of its use of Tor and crypto. It's arguable that Silk Road played a significant role in Bitcoin's early adoption (after all, it gave people a reason to use Bitcoin, albeit an illicit one). However, law enforcement was not amused. Various agencies (FBI, DEA, IRS, Secret Service) were on the case, and it turned into one of the most fascinating cat-and-mouse games of the cyber age.

By 2013, the Feds had made breakthroughs. Through old-fashioned investigative work and some slips by Ross (he famously posted on a public forum asking a programming question, using his personal email, about the Tor server setup – oops), they managed to pin Dread Pirate Roberts to Ross Ulbricht. The challenge was catching him red-handed while logged in as admin on Silk Road, so he couldn't hit an "encrypt & delete" button at the last second. In October 2013, agents tracked Ross to a public library in San Francisco. In a cinematic move, one agent pretended to be a feuding couple with another agent to distract Ross, and as he looked away, they snatched his open laptop from him. Boom: they had the admin account live and all the evidence.

Silk Road was promptly shut down. The site greeted visitors with an FBI seizure notice. The **FBI seized about 26,000 BTC from the site's escrow**

wallets. More startlingly, Ross's laptop contained the keys to a treasure trove of **144,000 BTC** (the commissions he had amassed from running Silk Road). All told, around **170,000 BTC** ended up in U.S. government hands. Back then, Bitcoin was ~$100 each, so it was "only" tens of millions of dollars. Little did they know those bitcoins would be worth billions later (the government auctioned most off in 2014 for around $334 each – one venture capitalist famously scooped up a bunch on the cheap; by 2021 those coins were worth over 100x more).

Ross Ulbricht's downfall was a huge news story. Depending on who you asked, he was either a libertarian hero or a criminal mastermind. In 2015, he was convicted on multiple counts (money laundering, drug trafficking, hacking-related charges, and being the kingpin of a criminal enterprise). The judge threw the book at him: **two life sentences + 40 years, without parole**. Essentially, he's set to die in prison unless he ever gets a presidential pardon (which some supporters loudly advocate for). The sentence was shockingly harsh to many – even some who agreed he should be punished felt that was extreme for a non-violent offender. The judge cited alleged murder-for-hire plots (there were claims Ross had tried to have some associates killed, though those charges were never separately tried) as a reason for no leniency.

From a crypto perspective, the Silk Road saga was a double-edged sword. It proved that Bitcoin could facilitate transactions that governments couldn't easily censor – which is part of crypto's ethos of freedom – but it also tied Bitcoin's image to black markets and crime in the public eye for years. Every other mainstream media article about Bitcoin would mention drug deals or Silk Road, much to the frustration of legitimate Bitcoin enthusiasts.

There were also ironic twists. For instance, two U.S. agents involved in the Silk Road case went rogue and stole bitcoins during the investigation – because apparently temptation is strong when you're literally looking at the private keys to millions. They were later caught and convicted themselves. Crime within the crime-fighters! You can't make this stuff up. Also, years later (2020), a hacker who had stolen a chunk of Silk Road bitcoins back in 2013 was identified by law enforcement using blockchain analysis, leading to another seizure of nearly 70,000 BTC. So, the U.S. Treasury got another unexpected bitcoin windfall thanks to Silk Road long after it was gone.

> **Crypto-Wojak:** *"I remember browsing Silk Road out of curiosity back in the day (for research purposes, of course!). It felt like the dark alley of the internet. Part of me thought, 'This is groundbreaking.' Another part thought, 'This is gonna end badly.' Spoiler: the second part was right."*

Silk Road's shutdown was a major turning point. It showed that **Bitcoin is not truly anonymous** – it's pseudonymous. With enough effort, blockchain forensics can link transactions to real identities, especially when criminals make operational security mistakes (which they almost always do at some point). It also underscored that law enforcement was not clueless about crypto; they adapted quickly. The FBI and friends effectively said, "We're watching, even on the dark web."

After Silk Road, a host of copycat markets rose (Silk Road 2.0, Agora, AlphaBay, etc.). Most of them eventually got busted too, often faster than the original. It became a bit of a whack-a-mole. One might say the "crypto fails" here were the assumptions by criminals that crypto made them untouchable. Time and again, that proved false.

From the perspective of Ulbricht and Silk Road users, this was a massive fail: the ultimate illicit startup going down in flames. For the FBI and justice system, it was a big win. For Bitcoin, arguably a PR win (distancing from crime) but short-term PR mess (sensational headlines). Regardless, it's one of the most dramatic episodes in crypto lore.

Fail-o-Meter: 8/10 (As a criminal enterprise, it was wildly "successful" until it very much wasn't. The audacity and scale make it legendary, but ultimately it was a colossal fail for those involved – ending in arrests and lost fortunes.)

Lessons Learned:

- *Bitcoin Isn't Anonymous, It's Traceable* – Every Bitcoin transaction is recorded on a public ledger. With clever analysis (and if you slip up by linking your identity somewhere), investigators can follow the money. Criminals who thought Bitcoin was a perfect cloak were proven wrong. If you need true anonymity, Bitcoin by itself won't guarantee it (there are privacy coins, but that's another story).

- *Crime Doesn't Pay (Especially in Crypto)* – The Silk Road saga is basically a high-tech cops-and-robbers tale that ended the way most drug kingpin stories do: with the kingpin behind bars. Just because a new technology emerges (like crypto or the dark web) doesn't mean the old rules don't apply. Law enforcement catches up eventually.
- *Don't Mix Personal Life with Secret Identities* – Ross's few operational security mistakes (like using his personal email in contexts related to Silk Road) gave investigators openings. The takeaway: even if you think you're being super stealthy online, one or two small mistakes can unravel everything. (Not that we're advising on how to be a better criminal, but it's a cautionary principle for privacy in general.)
- *The Government Can Become a Whale* – In crypto, a "whale" is someone with a huge amount of coins. Ironically, through seizures, governments can become whales. They then auction or sell coins, which can impact markets. So, big enforcement actions can have side-effects on crypto prices and distribution of coins.
- *Crypto is a Tool – Good or Bad Depends on Users* – Silk Road demonstrated that crypto can enable both noble ideals (resistance to censorship, financial freedom) and facilitate wrongdoing (drug trade, etc.). It's a neutral tool. The fail here was in the naive belief that "crypto + Tor = invincible criminal empire." The success was in showing the world both the power and limits of using crypto in the dark web context. The dual nature of technology is something every crypto user should understand – it can empower, but it doesn't exempt anyone from real-world consequences.

8

BitConnect – The Ponzi Scheme That Became a Meme

If you were around in the crypto scene in 2017, just hearing the word

"BitConnect" likely triggers either a shudder or a laugh (or both). **BitConnect** has since become the prime example of a crypto Ponzi scheme – notorious not just for defrauding a lot of people, but also for spawning one of the most iconic memes in crypto history. Yes, we're talking about *that guy* enthusiastically shouting "BitConnneeeeeect!!!"

First, what was BitConnect? It launched in 2016 as a cryptocurrency and a lending platform. The pitch was that you could **lend your Bitcoin to BitConnect's program** and earn insanely high interest – up to 1% *per day*! They claimed to have a "secret trading bot" that made profits to pay all investors. (Spoiler: there was no magical bot that could guarantee 1% daily gains. It was effectively a classic Ponzi: paying early users with money from new users.) To participate, you had to convert your Bitcoin into BitConnect's own token (called BCC) and then lock it on their platform for a period. They also had a referral program, so recruiting others got you bonuses – multi-level-marketing meets crypto.

Despite many savvy folks raising alarm bells (if it quacks like a Ponzi and walks like a Ponzi...), BitConnect grew like wildfire during the 2017 crypto boom. The BCC token even cracked the top 10 cryptos by market cap at one point. A lot of average Joes, not very experienced in crypto, got sucked in by the allure of easy riches and the social media hype. BitConnect promoters were everywhere on YouTube, flaunting how much interest they were earning and urging people to join the "financial revolution."

The pinnacle of BitConnect's hype was an event in January 2018 in Thailand – basically a big celebratory conference for the community. And there, on stage, came a man who would become a legend: **Carlos Matos** from New York. Carlos grabbed the mic in front of a pumped-up crowd and delivered a feverishly excited testimonial about BitConnect. He started by shouting "Hey hey hey!" and "What's up, what's up, what's up BitConnect!" with the energy level of someone who had way too much coffee (or perhaps something stronger). He proceeded to proclaim "I love BitConnect!" and told the story of how he was skeptical at first but then started seeing daily profits. The highlight was his drawn-out, exuberant scream of *"BIIIIITCONNEEEEEECT!!!"* which echoed through the hall.

Little did he know, he was birthing a meme. That clip of Carlos's over-the-top enthusiasm went viral in crypto circles (and beyond). It was remixed into songs, autotuned, used as a ringtone – you name it. He became the face of BitConnect, though he was just an investor and not actually running it. At that moment, BitConnect's reputation teetered between "maybe legit, maybe scam" and "this is some cultish goofy stuff" for many onlookers.

And then, *crash.* By late January 2018, just days after that big event, BitConnect collapsed spectacularly. Regulators in Texas and North Carolina had issued cease-and-desist letters, essentially calling BitConnect out as an unauthorized securities offering (and likely a Ponzi). Sensing the heat, BitConnect suddenly announced it was shutting down its lending program. Panic ensued. The BCC token's price, which had been hovering around $400, **plummeted to under $1** in a matter of days. Cue thousands of shocked investors realizing that all those on-paper profits were gone – poof – just like that.

It turned out exactly as skeptics predicted: BitConnect was a Ponzi scheme all along. Early investors who cashed out made money, but a lot of people who came in late lost everything they put in. Estimates suggest **over $2.5 billion** was swindled globally. Law enforcement eventually got involved. The FBI and other agencies started investigations. In 2021-2022, the DOJ and SEC formally charged several people behind BitConnect, including one of the founders (an Indian citizen, Satish Kumbhani, who remains at large) and a top promoter in the US. Several YouTube promoters who shilled BitConnect also got sued by investors and were probed by the SEC. It was a mess.

But what most remember is the meme. The absurdity of Carlos Matos's speech became symbolic of the irrational exuberance of that era. Even today, you'll see "BITCOOOOONNECT" referenced whenever someone talks about obvious scams or gets overly hyped about a questionable project. It's a way of saying, "Careful, this smells like BitConnect 2.0."

Crypto-Wojak: "In Carlos voice: 'Hey hey hey!' – *sometimes I do that in the mirror to remind myself never to fall for a Ponzi again. We all had that one friend who almost put money in BitConnect (or worse, did). If it weren't so tragic, the memes alone would have made it comedic gold."*

It's worth noting that Carlos himself later said he had no idea it was a scam; he was just really excited about the money he was making (on paper). After the crash, he became sort of an unwilling meme celebrity. There were rumors he lost a lot too, though he mostly stayed out of the spotlight after his 15 minutes of fame.

BitConnect's collapse did have a silver lining: it likely saved many newbies from falling for similar schemes afterwards, at least for a while. It became the cautionary tale that educators and influencers would cite: "Don't be like those BitConnect folks. If someone promises guaranteed high returns, run the other way!" Essentially, BitConnect walked (off a cliff) so that future investors might walk away from similar scams.

However, as crypto history shows, new Ponzi schemes pop up regularly (OneCoin, which we'll get to next, or various DeFi yield farms that turned out to be Ponzi-like). There's something about human greed and gullibility – it repeats. But BitConnect will forever remain the poster child, complete with its own theme soundbite.

Fail-o-Meter: 9/10 (A multi-billion dollar Ponzi that imploded, stranding investors worldwide, plus an immortal meme as its legacy. It loses a point only because, admit it, the meme was entertaining even if the scam was awful.)

Lessons Learned:

- *If Returns Are Unrealistically High and "Guaranteed," It's Probably a Scam* – BitConnect promised ~1% per day, which means your money could double in like 3 months, guaranteed. That's absurd. In any investment, such claims should set off alarm bells. In crypto, there's lots of volatility, but nothing legitimate can promise steady huge gains with no risk.
- *Beware the Cult Marketing and Referral Hype* – BitConnect's gatherings with chanting and its multi-level referral structure are classic Ponzi indicators. Real investments don't usually require you to recruit new people to get

paid or have leaders leading cheers about how rich you'll all be. If you see a cult-like atmosphere, get skeptical quick.

- *Do Your Research (DYOR) and Heed Red Flags* – Many in the crypto community did call out BitConnect as a Ponzi early on. There were Reddit threads, Twitter warnings, etc. Unfortunately, many newbies either didn't see them or ignored them. The lesson: before throwing money into a crypto platform, especially one that sounds magical, do some digging. If respected voices are screaming "scam," take that seriously.

- *Memes Can Be Educational* – The BitConnect meme, while funny, also served as a viral PSA. It helped spread awareness of the absurdity of the scheme. In a weird way, that meme probably prevented other people from investing, once they realized "wait, why is this thing a joke now?" Sometimes humor and ridicule can shine a light on truth that straightforward warnings might not.

- *Cash Out Profits; Don't Reinvest Everything* – Some BitConnect investors actually made profits (especially if they got in early). The smart ones took profits out. The greedy ones kept reinvesting their "interest" to compound more – and got burned when it collapsed. It's a reminder: if you ever find yourself in something that's making money and you suspect it might not last, take at least your initial investment (if not more) off the table. Don't be the one left holding the bag.

9

OneCoin – The Fake Crypto Pyramid and the Vanishing Cryptoqueen

If BitConnect was a visible implosion, **OneCoin** was a slow-burning, audacious scam that swindled people around the globe – and its mastermind literally disappeared into thin air. This is the story of a cryptocurrency that never actually existed, a multi-billion dollar pyramid scheme, and a woman now known as the "Missing Cryptoqueen."

OneCoin started around 2014, founded by **Ruja Ignatova**, a Bulgarian businesswoman with a flair for drama. Dr. Ruja (she had a Ph.D., adding to her allure) presented herself as a visionary bringing cryptocurrency to the masses. She would dress in glamorous gowns, speak on massive stages at OneCoin events with thousands of attendees, and proclaim that OneCoin was the "Bitcoin Killer" that would make early investors insanely wealthy. She was charismatic, polished, and convincing – so much so that from 2014 to 2017, an estimated **$4 billion** (yes, with a B) poured in from people buying into OneCoin packages.

Ah, yes, the packages: OneCoin didn't have a public sale on exchanges. Instead, it sold "educational packages" to people, ranging from a few hundred to tens of thousands of euros, which included some tokens that could be "mined" into OneCoins on their private system. It was basically a multi-level marketing (MLM) scheme. Recruiters earned commissions for bringing in new buyers. The more expensive package you bought, the more OneCoin "points" you got. They had their own internal exchange where, on paper, OneCoin's value kept rising. But – and this is crucial – **OneCoin had no real blockchain**. You couldn't actually withdraw your OneCoins to an external wallet. You couldn't trade them on any open market. All you had was a number in a database controlled entirely by OneCoin headquarters. In essence, it was a giant **excel sheet "cryptocurrency"**.

Despite this obvious red flag (no real blockchain, for a supposed crypto), millions of people from over 175 countries fell for it. Why? Well, many were not technically savvy and took Ruja's word. The promise of getting in early on the "next Bitcoin" was enticing. Plus, the MLM structure meant friends and family were recruiting each other – trust was leveraged. OneCoin targeted communities often overlooked by traditional finance, promising financial revolution.

By mid-2016, some regulators and analysts started calling out OneCoin as a likely scam. Warnings were issued in countries like Bulgaria, Finland, and later India (where some OneCoin promoters were arrested). But OneCoin kept operating, often just shifting its activities to regions with less oversight.

The dramatic climax came in October 2017. OneCoin was planning to go public (whatever that meant in their case) and Ruja Ignatova was scheduled to speak at a big event in Lisbon. She never showed. Literally vanished. Weeks turned into months; rumors swirled that she had fled with a stash of cash and possibly Bitcoin (it's alleged she converted a lot of OneCoin money into BTC). She left behind her co-founder (a guy named Sebastian Greenwood) and her younger brother **Konstantin Ignatov** to manage the fallout. Konstantin tried to keep OneCoin going, but the cracks were too wide. By early 2018, the whole scheme was crumbling as investigators closed in and people realized withdrawals weren't happening.

Ruja Ignatova's disappearance is one for the crime novels. She has been **on the run since 2017**. The FBI added her to their Top Ten Most Wanted list in 2022, and there's a $100,000 reward for information leading to her arrest. There are theories galore: some say she had plastic surgery and is hiding in plain sight; others think she might have been killed by accomplices. She's been dubbed the "Cryptoqueen" in media – partly out of morbid fascination that someone could orchestrate such a massive scam and then pull an actual vanishing act. There's even a popular BBC podcast titled **"The Missing Cryptoqueen"** that dives deep into the saga.

Meanwhile, legal consequences hit those who were caught. Konstantin Ignatov (her brother) was arrested in the U.S. in 2019 while ironically giving a talk about OneCoin (the audacity!). He pleaded guilty to fraud and money laundering and has been cooperating with authorities – he hasn't been sentenced yet, likely in exchange for info. Sebastian Greenwood (co-founder) was arrested in 2018 and later extradited to the U.S.; he's facing charges too. A bunch of other OneCoin operatives have faced charges in various countries. But Ruja – the mastermind – remains elusive.

From a victims' perspective, OneCoin was devastating. People from all walks of life were duped. Many stories emerged of folks mortgaging homes or borrowing to invest in OneCoin, only to lose it all. Unlike BitConnect, where at least some got their money out before the crash, OneCoin gave almost no one that chance, because you couldn't really cash out (aside from maybe selling some internal tokens to new victims within their system until that stopped). It was a slow rug-pull; by the time most realized something was wrong, the money had been siphoned away.

OneCoin's fail is unique because it wasn't a failure of technology (like the DAO hack) or an exchange hack (like Mt. Gox) – it was a failure of trust and human due diligence on a grand scale. It capitalized on crypto excitement but delivered nothing of the kind. It was basically a get-rich-quick scheme wearing crypto clothing.

> **Crypto-Wojak:** *"Imagine buying what you think are crypto coins, but there's no wallet, no blockchain explorer, nothing. Just glossy brochures and a charismatic founder. That's a whole new level of getting rekt. At least if I lose money trading a real coin, I know there was a coin! OneCoin victims didn't even get a coin – just an illusion."*

The OneCoin saga underscores a harsh truth: **if you don't understand how a crypto works, and you're just taking someone's word for it, you're playing with fire.** This scam targeted folks who largely didn't grasp blockchain tech – and the scammers used lots of crypto buzzwords to create a veneer of legitimacy. They even used the fact that Bitcoin was hard to understand as part of their pitch: "Bitcoin is too complex; OneCoin is the user-friendly version for everyone!" Oof.

In retrospect, OneCoin had myriad red flags: no verifiable tech, cult-like seminars, pressure to buy more packages, leaders flaunting extreme wealth (Ruja bought expensive properties, art, and even had a yacht reportedly named "The Davina"). But as is often the case, many victims ignored these until it was too late, caught up in the fear of missing out on the "next big thing."

OneCoin will go down in history as one of the largest frauds in the crypto space (if not the largest, by amount taken). It's a stark reminder that sometimes the biggest "crypto fail" is not a bug or a hack – it's a plain old fraud dressed up in techno-jargon.

Fail-o-Meter: 10/10 (An entirely fake cryptocurrency, billions stolen, and the mastermind disappearing like a puff of smoke. This is a gold-medal scam fail with enduring mystery to boot.)

Lessons Learned:

- *No Blockchain, No Real Coin* – If a cryptocurrency project doesn't have a transparent, working blockchain or network that you can independently verify, it's not a cryptocurrency; it's likely a scam. OneCoin literally had no blockchain. Always insist on actual technical substance: a whitepaper, open-source code, block explorers, etc.
- *Don't Fall for Titles and Glitz* – Dr. Ruja's Oxford education, her glamorous events, the term "cryptocurrency" thrown around – all that gave OneCoin an air of credibility. Scam artists often use appearances and credentials to lower skepticism. Evaluate the opportunity, not just the person selling it. Even a PhD can be a con artist (as sad as that is).
- *If You Can't Withdraw or Trade Freely, Be Very Afraid* – OneCoin trapped people's money by not allowing real withdrawals (beyond a closed ecosystem). Any legitimate project will allow you to control your assets (especially in crypto, where decentralization is key). If you're ever told, "you can buy in, but you can't sell yet" or "you can only sell on our internal platform," that's a red flag the size of a barn.
- *MLM + Crypto = Double Danger* – Multi-level marketing schemes are notorious on their own for often devolving into pyramids. Add crypto buzz to that and you have a potent scam cocktail. Be extremely wary of any crypto that heavily emphasizes recruiting others or selling packages rather than actual technology or usage.
- *Educate Yourself* – OneCoin preyed on lack of knowledge. The best defense for would-be crypto investors is education. You don't need to be a coder, but learn the basics of how legitimate cryptocurrencies work (public ledger, decentralized validation, etc.). Then scams like OneCoin stand out like a sore thumb. In crypto, knowledge truly is power – and protection.

10

FailCoin – When a Joke Coin Got the Last Laugh

Sometimes truth is stranger than fiction, and nowhere is that more evident than in the tale of **FailCoin**. Picture this: a traditional bank employee, fed up with all the crypto hoopla, decides to prove that the whole thing is a sham. To expose how gullible the market is, he creates a completely worthless cryptocurrency as a joke... only to watch in astonishment as the internet ironically pumps its value to the moon. What was meant to be a cautionary demonstration turned into a comedic case of **"Well, that backfired!"**.

Our story's protagonist (let's call him **Dan** – a composite character of a few real-life anecdotes) works at a bank and has long been a crypto skeptic. He's tired of hearing his friends and colleagues rave about dog coins and magic internet money. One evening, after yet another debate with a crypto-bro about how "everything is just speculation," Dan decides to make a point. He knows a bit of coding, enough to create a basic token on a blockchain. So he whips up a new token in an afternoon. He tongue-in-cheek names it **FailCoin (FAIL)**, because he fully expects (and intends) it to fail. Its purpose? Absolutely none. Its value? Zilch. Dan creates a million FAIL tokens, keeps some, and posts the rest on a decentralized exchange for practically free.

But he doesn't stop there. With a mischievous glint in his eye, Dan writes an anonymous post on a forum and a sarcastic tweet or two saying: "Here it is, folks: **FailCoin** – a coin that does nothing! Totally worthless! Don't buy it (unless you want to prove me right about how dumb crypto is)." He expects maybe a few chuckles and for it to die in obscurity. Instead... the internet grabs hold of it like a shiny new toy.

Some crypto degens on Twitter and Reddit stumble upon FailCoin. They see the reverse psychology humor in it. "Ha, someone made a coin literally called FAIL? Challenge accepted!" In a sort of memetic rally, people start buying small amounts as a joke, posting memes like "Going to the moon by failing upwards!" and "Bought some FAIL because why not YOLO." A community forms ironically around this anti-coin. Within 48 hours, FAIL's price, which was effectively near zero, shoots up thousands of percent. Suddenly, FailCoin has a market capitalization of several million dollars – on paper.

Dan is flabbergasted. The whole point was to show that random cryptos are worthless, and here are people trading his worthless crypto and driving its price up. Did they miss the memo? It's literally called FailCoin! He hops online in disbelief, telling folks, "Stop! This is a JOKE. It's not worth anything!" But, predictably, in the wild world of crypto, that only adds fuel. Now the narrative shifts: "The creator says it's worthless – must be trying to shake us out so he can buy more! HODL!" Some think Dan's dire warnings are actually reverse psychology or an attempt to get the price to dip so he can accumulate. Others fully understand it's a joke but keep trading it for giggles, trying to make a quick buck off the hype before it inevitably crashes.

For a brief, bizarre moment, FailCoin becomes an internet sensation. Its logo (a sinking ship with FAIL on the flag) is shared widely. One wag on Twitter quips, "FailCoin is the first project to succeed by failing successfully." Another jokes, "I invested in FAIL and all I got was this ironic sense of accomplishment." Even major news outlets catch wind – with headlines like **"Worthless 'Joke' Cryptocurrency Hits $50 Million Market Cap – Creator Throws Up Hands"**. Some compare it to historical anecdotes like the Dutch Tulip Mania or more directly to that time a TikToker created a coin literally named SCAM as a parody and it hit a $70 million market cap within an hour. The line between parody and reality in crypto has never been thinner.

After a few surreal weeks, reality does its thing: the joke wears off. Perhaps a bigger, newer meme distracts the crowds (there's always another shiny object in crypto). People start selling their FailCoin holdings, mostly laughing all the way out – some made a bit of money, others maybe lost a little if they bought near the top of this absurd spike. Dan, who at one point saw his own stash of FAIL (which he kept purely for demonstration) become worth a life-changing sum, may or may not have cashed out a bit. (If he did, oh the irony: his stunt to disprove crypto ended up making him profit, proving maybe he didn't understand human nature as well as he thought!) Eventually, FailCoin's price plummets back toward zero as expected. It lives on only as a quirky anecdote and a footnote in the annals of crypto craziness.

So, what's the moral here? On one hand, Dan's initial point was validated – people really will throw money at almost anything in a speculative frenzy. On the other hand, the episode also shows the other side of that coin: a community can form around even the silliest idea, and **perceived** value (even if rooted in satire) can temporarily trump logic. In a way, the FailCoin saga became a self-aware parody of crypto mania – with participants in on the joke even as they were the butt of the joke.

> **Crypto-Wojak:** *"I totally bought some FailCoin during that whole meme-stock-meets-crypto moment. Not my proudest trade, but I made enough for a nice dinner before it tanked. I mean, when the universe hands you a meme, sometimes you ride it for the lulz."*

FailCoin might be fictional in name (though similar real incidents have occurred), but the lessons it illustrates are very real. We've reached a point where a token explicitly advertised as worthless can attract millions in investment short-term. It's equal parts humorous and humbling. For seasoned crypto folks, it's a facepalm reminder of the speculative excesses that can grip the market. For outsiders, it's an example they cite to claim crypto is just a fool's game. For participants, it was kind of a communal joke – a way to thumb their nose at stuffy financiers by saying, "Look, we know this is silly money – but we're having fun, and some of us will even profit from the greater fools."

In the end, FailCoin did indeed fail – as intended – but not before becoming a spectacular success of sorts. Its rise and fall lasted maybe a month in total, but it perfectly encapsulated the chaotic humor of the crypto world.

Fail-o-Meter: 7/10 (Not a catastrophic loss like others, more of a comedic fail. The market's irrationality was the joke, and everyone got the punchline eventually.)

Lessons Learned:

- *The Market Can Stay Irrational Longer Than You Can Stay Sane* – Just because something has no fundamental value doesn't mean people won't buy it. In crypto, especially in bull runs, **anything** can pump. Don't assume rational behavior in the short term. As the saying goes, "markets can be irrational longer than you can remain solvent" – so shorting a meme might wreck you before sanity returns.

- *Meme Power is Real* – Never underestimate the power of a good meme or a humorous narrative in crypto. People sometimes invest in the narrative or joke as much as in any fundamentals. Dogecoin started as a joke and became a top crypto. FOMO and collective humor can move mountains (of market cap), albeit temporarily.

- *Know When to Step Away* – If you ever find yourself involved in a purely speculative mania (and you know it), have the sense to take profits and get out before the crash. Many FailCoin-like episodes end with latecomers holding the bag. Enjoy the ride if you partake, but don't be greedy thinking the party will last forever.

- *Proving a Point May Prove the Opposite* – Our friend Dan learned that trying to "prove crypto is stupid" by engaging with it can produce paradoxical outcomes. Engaging with an ecosystem – even to mock it – can add fuel to it. The broader lesson: sometimes the best way to critique something is to simply avoid giving it energy. In crypto, satire can turn into actual value once the crowd gets hold of it.

- *Stay Humble and Amused* – Finally, the FailCoin story reminds us not to take ourselves (or the markets) too seriously. Crazy things happen. If you're in the crypto space, buckle up and keep a sense of humor. Today's ridiculous fad could be tomorrow's fortune (or vice versa). Being able to laugh at the absurdity can keep you grounded – just make sure you're laughing with a safety net and not betting the farm on a joke.

11

Bonus Chapter: Everyday Crypto Fails – Tales from the Trenches

Not all crypto fails make headlines. Many happen to regular folks in everyday situations – often teaching hard lessons (sometimes with a side of humor) to those of us navigating the blockchain jungle. In this bonus chapter, we'll look at a series of **relatable blunders** that crypto enthusiasts (new and seasoned alike) commonly experience. Think of these as cautionary tales that might save you from uttering the dreaded phrase, "I can't believe I just did that..."

Oops, Wrong Address!

You triple-check the long string of letters and numbers, hit send, and then... a sinking feeling: you just **sent your crypto to the wrong address**. This is a classic. Maybe you copied the address incorrectly or selected the wrong saved contact. Or perhaps you sent Ethereum to an Ethereum Classic address, or Bitcoin to a Bitcoin Cash address – an easy mistake when wallet interfaces are confusing. Unlike emailing the wrong person, there's usually no "Undo Send" in crypto. Those coins might be gone forever, lost in the abyss of someone else's wallet (if that wallet even has an owner; sometimes it's just an address with no private key – effectively a black hole). Every crypto old-timer has heard the horror stories: sending 2 BTC to a typo'd address and watching it disappear into the void, sending tokens on the wrong blockchain network and unable to retrieve them, or even **copy-paste fails** where malicious software alters the pasted address to an attacker's address (sneaky!).

The fail here is simple human error, amplified by the unforgiving nature of crypto. It's like sending a letter and writing the address slightly wrong – except the postal service can't help you, and the letter is full of cash. Some blockchain networks now have features to prevent this (like checksums or ENS domains – human-readable addresses), but many people still learn the hard way.

Lesson: Always double-check (then triple-check) the recipient address character by character. If possible, send a small test amount first. Use features like QR codes or saved address books carefully. And mentally prepare that if you do screw up, recovery is usually impossible – so caution is your best friend.

Lost Keys, Lost Coins

"One wallet to rule them all," you thought as you proudly moved your crypto off an exchange to your personal wallet. Not your keys, not your coins, right? So you made sure to be your own bank. But then tragedy: you **lost the private key or seed phrase** to your wallet. Maybe you wrote it on a piece of paper that your dog literally ate (it's happened). Or you saved it in a text file on a laptop that later fried. Perhaps you were absolutely sure you'd remember that 12-word seed phrase or that complex password – only to draw a complete blank when needed.

This kind of fail can be soul-crushing. Knowing that your digital fortune is sitting right there on the blockchain, but you can't access it because the keys are lost, is a special kind of torture. It's like being locked out of a safe that only you should have the combo to, and watching the contents through bulletproof glass. Recall the earlier chapter about James Howell's landfill hard drive – that's an extreme case. But everyday folks lose smaller amounts all the time this way. Forums are filled with pleas like, "I lost my recovery phrase, can I get my coins back?" and the sad answer is almost always, "Nope." There's no password reset in decentralized land.

Lesson: **Back up your keys/seed phrase in multiple secure ways.** Write them down (on paper or metal), store in a safe or safety deposit box. Use a hardware wallet that makes you back up a seed. Don't trust your memory alone. And never share those keys with anyone. Being your own bank is empowering until you realize you also have to be your own security team.

Rug Pulled by a Meme Coin

We all know FOMO (Fear Of Missing Out) is real in crypto. You hear about someone turning $100 into $100,000 on "FluffyDogeShib" coin, and you think, why not me? So you find the hottest **meme coin** on Twitter or a Telegram tip – let's call it *MoonHamster*. It's ultra new, everyone's hyping it with rocket emojis and "we're all gonna make it" chants. You throw some money in – after all, YOLO. For a day or two, the price actually shoots up! Your $500 is now $5,000 on paper. You start planning which color Lambo you'll buy.

Then one morning, *poof*. The coin's price plunges 99% in minutes. What happened? **Rug pull.** The anonymous developers behind MoonHamster inserted a malicious code that allows them to drain the liquidity or mint billions of new tokens for themselves. Or they simply sold their massive pre-mined stack all at once, crashing the market – basically pulling the rug out from under investors. You're left holding a bag of tokens that are now worth less than the gas fee you paid to buy them.

This kind of fail is a rite of passage for many a degen trader. It's the classic "greater fool" game and you realize with pain that you were not the greatest fool, but certainly a greater fool than you hoped. The signs were there (no project website, no audit, devs named "CryptoLord69" on Telegram who banned anyone asking legit questions), but the allure of quick gains muffled the warnings.

Lesson: The higher the potential reward, the higher the risk. **Do thorough research** before apeing into a new coin. If the project is anonymous, unaudited, has unclear tokenomics, or promises unreasonable returns, be cautious. If you do play in meme coin casino, never invest more than you can afford to lose in five minutes. And consider taking profits on the way up – don't diamond-hand a meme coin forever; very few reach Dogecoin longevity.

Falling for a Phishing Scam

Even the most careful crypto user can fall prey to a well-crafted **phishing scam**. One common scenario: you get an email that looks exactly like it's from your hardware wallet company or a crypto exchange you use. "Urgent Security Update Required," it says. Heart pounding a bit, you click the link, which takes you to what looks like the legitimate login page or app interface. Without thinking, you enter your seed phrase or password to "verify your account." And just like that, you handed the keys to a scammer.

Or maybe you googled a wallet's name and clicked the first link, not realizing it was a Google ad that led to a fake site. Or on Discord, a "support admin" DMed you offering help for an issue you mentioned in a server, and walked you through "fixing" it (which involved you giving up sensitive info). These phishers are crafty, and in the heat of the moment, even experienced folks have been duped. The result is usually immediate theft: the scammer sweeps your wallet of all assets. You watch, helpless and horrified, as your funds get sent to an unknown address.

Phishing is basically the crypto equivalent of someone conning you into giving them your house keys and alarm code. It's low-tech hacking: hacking the human, not the system. And it happens every day.

Lesson: **Never ever enter your seed phrase or private key unless you are 100% sure why and with whom.** No legitimate support will ever ask for your seed phrase – that's a huge red flag. Double-check URLs for exchanges or wallet sites (look for the padlock, verify the spelling). Be suspicious of unsolicited messages. Use bookmarks for important sites rather than clicking links. And if something smells phishy, stop and verify through official channels. In crypto, being paranoid can save your assets.

FOMO and Panic – Buy High, Sell Low

Our final everyday fail is a tale as old as markets themselves: the vicious cycle of **FOMO and panic**. It goes like this – you see Bitcoin or another coin skyrocketing. It's all over the news: "Bitcoin up 200% this month!" Everyone on social media is euphoric. You feel late to the party, but you can't resist anymore. So you **buy in at the peak**, because better late than never, right? For a moment, it even keeps going up, affirming your decision. But then the trend reverses (as cycles do). The price starts dipping... then dropping... oh no, now it's cratering. Your investment is down 30%, 40%... Fear kicks in. You've seen this movie before – maybe in 2018 or some other crash – and you panic. In a flurry of anxiety, you **sell at the bottom** to salvage what's left.

Congratulations, you just locked in losses – essentially doing the opposite of the classic wisdom "buy low, sell high." You're not alone; many people do exactly this. It's practically a meme: the inexperienced trader who buys the top and sells the bottom. Emotions are powerful drivers. FOMO (the greed of not missing out on gains) pushes you to buy high, and panic (the fear of losing it all) pushes you to sell low. The result: a shrinking portfolio and a lesson in emotional control.

Perhaps the next week, the price recovers and even exceeds the point where you bought. Now you feel the sting twice – you lost money and if you'd just held, you'd be up. It's a brutal personal fail that can repeat until one learns to tame those emotions or use strategies like dollar-cost averaging or setting stop-loss orders rationally.

Lesson: **Have a plan and stick to it.** If you're investing, try to buy in stages, not when hype is at a peak. If you're trading, set clear levels for taking profit and cutting loss *before* emotions spike. Consider the timeless advice: be greedy when others are fearful and fearful when others are greedy (thank you, Warren Buffett). It's easier said than done, but recognizing the FOMO/panic loop is the first step to breaking it. In crypto, volatility is wild; steel your nerves or you'll be forever chasing your tail.

These everyday fails might not grab headlines like our Top 10 epic fails, but they are the kind of mistakes that collectively cost crypto users millions and plenty of heartache. The silver lining is that each usually happens only once to a person – because the pain teaches you quick. Make a misstep, say "well, that's never happening again," and adjust your approach.

If you cringed at any of these and thought, "Oh no, I did that," don't feel too bad. **Crypto-Wojak's** been there too – battle scars and all. The key is to learn and perhaps laugh about it later. After all, every expert was once a newbie who sent 0.1 BTC to the wrong address or aped into a doomed coin. It's all part of the journey through the blockchain jungle.

12

Conclusion

Laughing and Learning in the Crypto Jungle

What a journey it's been through the wilds of Crypto Land! We've navigated through ten of the greatest fails – from pizzas worth millions to vanishing billions, from hacked code to outright scams – and capped it off with some everyday oopsies that could happen to any of us. If there's one thing you should take away (besides maybe double-checking that wallet address before you hit send), it's that **the crypto world is as unpredictable as it is entertaining**. For every "moon" there's a "rekt", for every success a cautionary tale, and through it all, an irrepressible community that manages to meme its way through the chaos.

By now, you've seen that behind each epic fail is a lesson (or three) learned. We've laughed at Laszlo's expensive pizzas, but also appreciated the role it played in crypto history. We cringed at Mt. Gox and Quadriga, yet those failures prompted better security and the mantra of "not your keys, not your coins." We winced at Ponzi schemes and scams, but they taught thousands to be smarter next time (and gave us legendary memes like "Bitconnneeeeect!"). We watched a stablecoin become anything but stable, reinforcing that if something can go wrong in crypto, sometimes it will – and spectacularly so. And through Crypto-Wojak's snarky commentary, we hopefully found a friend who voiced our incredulity and our insider chuckles at how absurd things can get.

Crypto-Wojak, our intrepid guide, would like a final word:

> **Crypto-Wojak:** *"My portfolio's been through booms and busts, I've made and lost fortunes (on paper), and I've got the emotional scars of riding this rollercoaster – but you know what? I ain't leaving. Why? Because we're a weird, wonderful tribe and, deep down, I still believe: We're all gonna make it (WAGMI)... eventually, maybe, sort of. And even if not, at least we'll have some good stories to tell."*

That's the thing about this community – we cope with humor. When someone posts that they accidentally sent 20 ETH to a contract with no withdrawal function, the comments will be a mix of "ouch, sorry bro" and memes of Pepe crying. When the market tanks 30% in a day, Crypto Twitter floods with gifs of rollercoasters and jokes about "discount buying opportunities." It's a culture of turning pain into punchlines – not to minimize the losses (which are real), but to remind ourselves not to take any of this too personally. The blockchain doesn't care about our feelings; sometimes laughing is the only sane response.

As you close this book, consider this: **your own crypto stories are being written**. Maybe you'll never accidentally throw away a hard drive with a fortune (knock on wood), but you might fat-finger a trade or fall for a clever scam once. Maybe you'll never run an exchange that gets hacked, but you might experience that gut-punch when a coin you believed in goes to zero overnight. It's okay. It's all part of the grand experiment we're living through. The key is to stick around and learn. Over time, you'll likely find that your fails become fewer (and smaller), and your wins – whether financial or simply the win of *not making a dumb mistake you once would have* – become more frequent.

The crypto frontier is not for the faint of heart, but it's certainly never boring. And despite all the fails we've chronicled, let's not forget the resilience of this space. After Mt. Gox's collapse, Bitcoin didn't die – it grew stronger, inspiring a new generation of exchanges and believers. After The DAO hack, Ethereum didn't die – it adapted and became even more central to decentralized finance and NFTs (with "code is law" now tempered by caution). After Terra's implosion, the industry took a hard look at stablecoins, leading to more robust models. Every fail has, in some way, shaped the evolution of crypto – often for the better, even if painfully so.

So here's to the risk-takers, the degens, the builders, the hodlers, and yes, even the skeptics – because a healthy dose of skepticism helps keep us safe. May you navigate the blockchain jungle with a bit more wisdom and a lot more humor.

And hey, if you ever experience a crypto fail of your own, don't be too shy to share it. In this community, there's a good chance others will chime in with "been there, done that," and you might even get a meme or two out of it. In fact, consider this an open invitation: share your wildest crypto fail stories on social media (use a fun hashtag like **#CryptoFail** or tag our friend **Crypto-Wojak** if he ever gets a Twitter account). Not only will it be cathartic, but you'll be contributing to the collective knowledge (and amusement) of the community. After all, laughter is the best medicine – especially when your portfolio is bleeding red.

Thank you for coming along on this ride through the highs and lows of cryptopia. Keep learning, stay safe (but keep your sense of adventure), and never lose your ability to laugh at the absurdity we're all witnessing in real time. Who knows – maybe years from now, you'll be telling a newbie about "that time in 2025 when [insert crazy event] happened," as they shake their head in disbelief. The cycle continues, and you'll have graduated from rookie to wise old crypto owl, complete with your own collection of battle stories.

Until then, stay meme-worthy, my friends. And remember: **Don't Panic (and HODL)** – the crypto universe rewards those who endure... or at least it gives them great stories.

Happy trading, happy failing (productively), and see you on the moon – or in the next dip buying party!

www.ingramcontent.com/pod-product-compliance
Lightning Source LLC
LaVergne TN
LVHW051609050326
832903LV00033B/4424